Plant Based

Breakfast Favorites

Chef Julia Dunaway

No part of the publication may be reproduced, distributed, or transmitted in any form or by any means, or stored in a database or retrieval system, without the prior written permission of the publisher.

Text copyright © 2021 by Julia Dunaway
All Rights Reserved. Printed in the United States of America

Published by Motina Books, LLC, Van Alstyne, Texas
www.MotinaBooks.com

Names: Dunaway, Julia
Title: Plant Based Breakfast Favorites
Description: First Edition. | Van Alstyne: Motina Books, 2021
ISBN-13: 978-1-945060-52-6 (paperback)

Subjects: BISAC: COOKING / Vegetarian

Dedicated to my daughter, Alexandra Stokes, who helped me create this book. She introduced me to boxers, Macbook Pros, Stitchfix, Kate Spade, boba tea, and always keeps me on my toes. She's talented, hard working and much smarter than me. Love you, Alex.

Plant Based Breakfast Favorites - Recipes

About Me 1

Daily Greens 2

Daily Smoothie 3

Chocolate Smoothie 4

Oats & Grains 5

    Chilled Oatmeal with Apples 5

    Simple Overnight Oatmeal with Fruit 6

    Chocolate Oatmeal 6

    90 Second Oatmeal 7

    Cold Cereal + Oats 7

    Steel-Cut Oatmeal 8

    Old-Fashioned Oatmeal and Toppings 8

    4 Grain Breakfast Bowl 9

    Breakfast Porridge 9

    Steel-Cut Oat Porridge 10

    Cold Oatmeal 10

Pancakes & Waffles 11

    How to Keep Waffles from Sticking 12

    Almond Granola Waffle 13

    Nutty Multigrain Waffles 14

    Berry Compote 15

    Fluffy Whole Grain Pancakes 16

    Oatmeal Pancakes 17

    Nut & Grain Pancakes 18

    Pancake & Waffle Toppings 19

Baked Goods 20

    Walnut Crusted French Toast 21

    Almond Joy Baked Oatmeal 23

    Baked Oatmeal with Apples 24

    Baked Oatmeal for One 25

    Spelt Banana Bread 26

    Cashew Frosting 28

- Miso Glaze ... 28
- Pumpkin Bread with Miso Glaze ... 29
- My Favorite Granola ... 31
- Orange Ginger Almond Chocolate Oat Muffins ... 33
- Oatmeal Nut Butter Balls ... 35
- Oatmeal & Fruit Muffins ... 37
- Cinnamon Rolls ... 39
- Apple Crisp ... 41
- Fruit & Nut Bars ... 44
- Chocolate Peanut Butter Date Bars ... 46

Savory ... 48
- Vegetable Frittata ... 49
- Biscuits & Sausage Gravy ... 51
- WFPB Sausage ... 53
- Breakfast Tofu ... 55
- Avocado Toast ... 56
- Classic Tofu Scramble ... 57
- Hashbrown Casserole ... 58
- Creamy Grits ... 61
- Crispy, Pan-Fried Potatoes ... 62
- Savory Steel-Cut Oatmeal ... 63
- Breakfast Sandwich with Sausage, Savory Tofu & Cheese Sauce ... 65
- Sausage ... 65
- Savory Tofu ... 67
- Cheese Sauce ... 69
- Crispy Tofu Cubes ... 70

Southwestern + Tex-Mex ... 71
- Breakfast Tacos +Chipotle Tofu +Chipotle Aioli +Guacamole ... 72
- Chipotle Tofu ... 73
- Chipotle Aioli ... 74
- Guacamole ... 74
- Spicy Potatoes ... 75
- Hatch Green Chili Grits ... 76
- Hatch Green Chili Tofu Scramble ... 77
- Austin Breakfast Tacos+ Tofu Sausage ... 78

Japanese Breakfast 79
    Miso Soup 80
    Japanese Rice 82
    Japanese Breakfast Tofu 83
    Natto 84

About Me

Hi! I'm Chef Julia Dunaway, a plant-based chef who teaches cooking classes, mostly on-line since 2020, but eventually I'll be doing in-person classes again. I graduated from the Culinary School of Fort Worth in 2009 and have had my own chef business since then. I have an active YouTube Channel, enjoy doing weekly live videos on social media and love developing recipes.

My focus changed to the whole-food plant-based way of eating in 2017 and I never looked back. Despite eating a plant-based diet I was still overweight by 30 pounds, so in May 2020, I decided to get serious about the whole food plant-based no oil lifestyle. I cut out so called "plant-based" restaurant food (usually full of oil), processed vegan food, vegan desserts, and all the not-so-healthy foods than tend to creep into a plant-based diet. I started following the Daily Dozen plan by Dr. Michael Greger, from the book *How Not To Die*. I included 90 minutes of exercise a day, as well. I was finally able to lose the stubborn 30 pounds that wouldn't come off before and I've maintained my goal weight since then.

Breakfast is near and dear to my heart. I've always loved going out for breakfast and brunch, or making big hearty breakfasts on the weekend. Although I love oatmeal and eat it nearly every day, as you can tell by the number of oatmeal recipes in this e-book, I also love savory breakfasts. My tofu scrambles, grits, hash brown casserole, frittata, and breakfast tacos are perfect for weekend breakfast and brunch. Additionally, I had always enjoyed pancakes and waffles. How could I satisfy my craving for IHOP Harvest Nut & Grain pancakes? What about waffles? How could I make them without using oil on the waffle iron? How could I make biscuits and gravy? With a lot of trial and error, I messed up many times, but finally figured out ways to make my favorite foods in this new way. I hope you enjoy my versions of plant-based no oil breakfast dishes!

Daily Greens

INGREDIENTS

- 10 ounces "Power Greens" (kale, spinach, chard, etc.)
- Balsamic vinegar

INSTRUCTIONS

- Fill a bowl with water and add a cup of ice cubes.
- Bring 6 quarts of water to a boil.
- Add 10 ounces of power greens. Cook for 30 seconds
- Scoop them out and into a bowl of ice water. When cool, drain the greens in a colander. Squeeze the greens with your hands until all the water is squeezed out.
- Place ½ cup of the greens in a bowl and serve plain or drizzle with balsamic vinegar or Ume Plum Vinegar, low-sodium soy sauce and Eden Shake.

I eat at least two servings of greens a day, usually 4-6.

Greens are sold in many forms. Bunches of kale, spinach, chard work fine in this recipe but may take longer if mature. The giant 24 ounce bag of mixed "power greens" sold at Costco are convenient and grocery stores sell 10 ounce containers or bags of a mixture of kale, spinach, and chard. These are usually "baby" vegetables and cook very quickly. Another option is to grow your own kale, chard and greens.

Daily Smoothie

INGREDIENTS

- 1 cup organic plant milk of your choice (no added oil)
- 5 ice cubes
- ½ cup blueberries (or berry blend)
- ½ frozen banana
- 1 tbsp ground flax seed
- 1 tbsp chia seeds
- ½ tbsp hemp seeds
- 2 tbsp walnuts (optional)
- 1 tbsp goji berries
- 1 tbsp pumpkin seeds
- 1/2 tsp ginger
- 1/2 tsp turmeric
- 1 tsp Amla powder
- ½ tbsp matcha powder
- dash of freshly ground black pepper

INSTRUCTIONS

- Place the soy milk, banana, and 5 or 6 ice cubes in a high-speed blender, such as a Vitamix.
- Add the rest of the ingredients.
- Start on low power and increase gradually as ingredients combine.
- Once combined well, turn the speed to high.
- If the mixture is too thick, add a couple tablespoons of water.
- Pour into a 24-32 ounce container and drink right away.

Chocolate Smoothie

INGREDIENTS

- 1 cup soy milk (or any plant milk)
- 1 frozen banana
- ½ cup blueberries (frozen or fresh)
- 2 tablespoon cacao powder
- 1 tablespoon ground flax meal
- ½ teaspoon vanilla extract or vanilla paste
- 2 dates or 2 tablespoons date syrup
- 5 ice cubes
- Optional: 1/2 cup spinach or mixed greens

INSTRUCTIONS

- Place the soy milk, banana, and 5 or 6 ice cubes in a high-speed blender, such as a Vitamix.
- Add the rest of the ingredients.
- Start on low power and increase gradually as ingredients combine.
- Once combined well, turn the speed to high.
- If the mixture is too thick, add a couple tablespoons of water.
- Pour into a 24-32 ounce container and drink right away.

Oats & Grains

Chilled Oatmeal with Apples

INGREDIENTS

- 1 cup rolled oats
- 1 cup chopped apple, Kanzi, Gala, Pink Lady
- 1 cup plant milk (I like almond milk.)
- 2 dates, pitted and chopped
- 2 tablespoons chopped nuts
- 1 tablespoon date syrup (or maple)
- ¼ teaspoon ginger
- ½ teaspoon cinnamon
- Or 1 teaspoon Fresh Jax Maple

INSTRUCTIONS

- Mix all ingredients together and place in individual serving dishes or pint mason jars.
- Chill for a few minutes and up three or four days.
- This oatmeal tastes great right after you make it or as an overnight oatmeal.

Simple Overnight Oatmeal with Fruit

INGREDIENTS

- ½ cup whole (rolled) oats
- ½ cup plant milk
- Fresh berries or fruit of your choice
- 1 or 2 dates, chopped
- 1 tablespoon flax/chia/hemp seed mixture (optional)

INSTRUCTIONS

- Mix the oats with the milk. Add dates for sweetness, if desired. Add flax mixture. Stir well. Place in a jar or bowl. Add fruit, cover and chill overnight.
- Options: Add 1 tablespoon peanut butter or almond butter, sliced banana, drizzle with maple syrup.
- If you prefer your oatmeal hot, place it in the microwave for 1 minute.

Chocolate Oatmeal

INGREDIENTS

- ½ cup rolled oats
- ½ cup plant milk
- 1 tbsp cacao powder (Trader Joe's)
- 1 tsp date or maple syrup
- 1 tbsp vegan dark chocolate chips
- 1 tbsp almond butter (optional)
- 1 tbsp chopped almonds

INSTRUCTIONS

- Add ingredients (except chocolate chips) to a deep bowl. Microwave for 90 seconds.
- Add the dark chocolate chips and almond butter, along with the chopped almonds.
- Add additional plant milk, if desired

90 Second Oatmeal

INGREDIENTS

- ½ cup rolled oats
- ½ cup almond milk

INSTRUCTIONS

- Mix together and microwave for 90 seconds
- I add a little more non-dairy milk and whatever fruit I have and a sprinkle of My Favorite Granola (oil-free).

Cold Cereal + Oats

INSTRUCTIONS

I like to measure out ¼ cup each of 4 different cereals and serve with the almond milk and toppings

Cold cereal is fine for busy days, however, try to find the highest fiber cereal with no added sugar or oil. Beware that most cereals have way too much added sugar. There are only a few that are super low in sugar and have no added fat.

INGREDIENTS

- Uncle Sam's Cereal
- Ezekiel 4:9
- Muesli (Bob's Red Mill)
- Rolled oats
- Brown rice crispy cereal
- Rip's Big Bowl Cereal
- Almond Milk (or alt.)
- Bananas, Berries, Chopped Walnuts

Steel-Cut Oatmeal

INSTRUCTIONS

- Bring water to a boil, add oats and simmer on low heat uncovered for 15-25 minutes, or until desired level of chewiness. I stop at 15 minutes.
- Top with walnuts, granola, dried or fresh fruit, almond milk, and cinnamon.
- Pictured: steel cut oats with 1 tablespoon 70% dark chocolate, Roasted almonds, 1 tablespoon almond butter and a sprinkle of coconut with a little almond milk on top.

INGREDIENTS

- 3 cups water
- 1 cup steel-cut oats

Old-Fashioned Oatmeal and Toppings

INGREDIENTS

- 2 cups water
- 1 cup old-fashioned oatmeal

TOPPINGS

- Dried fruit
- Coconut flakes
- Granola

INSTRUCTIONS

- Bring water to a boil, add oats and simmer for 5 minutes.
- Nuts (Pecans, almonds, walnuts, cashews)
- Seeds (Pumpkin, sunflower, chia)
- Almond or peanut butter
- Chocolate chips (vegan)
- Fruit only jam
- Maple, coconut, or date syrup

4 Grain Breakfast Bowl

INGREDIENTS

2 servings

- ¼ cup hulled barley
- ¼ cup beluga lentils
- ¼ cup rye
- ¼ cup oats groats
- 2 cups water

INSTRUCTIONS

Instant Pot

- Cook at high pressure for 30 minutes, release for 10 minutes naturally, then fully release.
- Can substitute with other grains such as farro, steel cut oats, urad lentils, etc. Serve with greens.

Breakfast Porridge

INGREDIENTS 4 servings

- 3 cups almond milk
- ½ cup steel cut oats
- ¼ cup quinoa
- ¼ cup 7 grain mix (Nishiki brand) or ¼ cup millet
- Pinch of salt

INSTRUCTIONS

- Place the quinoa and 7 grain mix or millet in a fine mesh strainer and rinse well.
- Bring the almond milk to a boil. Add the steel cut oats and quinoa/grain mix/millet. Reduce to a simmer and cook for 35-40 minutes or until done. The porridge should have a slightly chewy texture. Add a little water if it becomes too thick.
- Serve with almond milk, sliced bananas, strawberries, blueberries, blackberries, and a couple chopped almonds. Sprinkle with hemp seeds, flaxseed meal or chia seeds.

Steel-Cut Oat Porridge

INGREDIENTS 3 servings

- 3 cups water
- 1 cup almond milk
- 1 whole cinnamon stick
- ¼ teaspoon kosher salt
- 1 cup steel cut oats

INSTRUCTIONS

- Bring the water, milk and cinnamon stick to a boil in a medium saucepan.
- Stir in the oats. Return to a boil. Reduce heat and partially cover the pan. Cook until the oats are tender but still have some texture, about 20 minutes.
- Discard cinnamon stick. Serve with sliced bananas, nuts, and dates. Sprinkle with ground flax seeds and drizzle with additional almond milk.

Cold Oatmeal

INSTRUCTIONS

Rolled oats do not have to be cooked at all. You can eat them with fruit and milk like you would a cold cereal.

Pancakes & Waffles

How to Keep Waffles from Sticking

I have a new waffle iron that has not been used with any sprays or oils. It is completely non-stick and works well. If you start using sprays and oils it is almost impossible to make non-stick, no oil waffles and pancakes. The griddle works fine without sprays and oils, just make sure to cook the pancakes until they are done or they will be hard to turn over.

Almond Granola Waffle

INGREDIENTS

- 1 ¼ cups whole wheat pastry flour or spelt flour
- ½ cup almond meal
- ½ teaspoon baking powder
- Pinch of sea salt
- 2-3 tablespoons turbinado sugar (or date sugar)
- ½ teaspoon cinnamon or 1 tablespoon Fresh Jax Maple Cinnamon sprinkle
- 1 cup almond milk
- ½ cup apple sauce
- 1 tablespoon maple syrup
- 1 flax egg (1 tablespoon ground flax seed mixed with 3 tablespoons water)
- ½ cup homemade granola (See My Favorite Granola recipe.) OR
- ½ cup chopped nuts (walnuts, almonds, pecans)

INSTRUCTIONS

Mix the whole wheat pastry flour, almond flour, baking powder, sea salt, sugar and cinnamon together and use a whisk to mix it together well.

In a separate bowl, combine the almond milk, apple sauce, maple syrup, and flax egg and mix well. Add all the dry ingredients (except granola) to the wet ingredients and mix until just combined well. Don't over mix. Add the granola or nuts and stir.

Heat the waffle iron. Place about ½ cup or more batter on the hot waffle iron (depending on the size of your waffle iron). Cook about 3 minutes per side.

Serve with sliced strawberries, blackberries, sliced almonds, almond yogurt, and more granola sprinkled on top.

Nutty Multigrain Waffles

INGREDIENTS

- 1 cup Bob's Red Mill multigrain pancake/waffle mix (oil and dairy-free type)
- ½ cup whole wheat pastry flour
- ¼ cup almond meal (flour)
- 2 tablespoons ground flax seed
- 1 tablespoon baking powder
- ¼ teaspoon kosher salt
- ¼ cup dry sweetener of your choice (cane sugar, date sugar, coconut sugar or 4 Medjool dates soaked in liquid and drained)
- ½ teaspoon cinnamon
- 1 cup finely chopped walnuts
- 4 tablespoons aquafaba or 2 flax eggs (1 flax egg = 1 tablespoon ground flax seeds mixed with 2 ½ tablespoons water)
- 2 cups unsweetened soy milk

INSTRUCTIONS

- Mix dry ingredients together. In a separate bowl, mix together the wet ingredients. Combine.
- Heat a waffle iron and add about 1 cup of batter when it's at the proper temperature. My waffle maker lights up when it's ready.
- Cook until the waffle iron indicates it's ready (beep) or after about 3 minutes, depending on your waffle iron. Open slowly and use a wooden skewer to gently pry the waffle off the iron.
- Serve with Berry Compote.
- For Chocolate Waffles add ¼ cup cocoa powder and ½ cup chopped vegan chocolate to dry ingredients.

Berry Compote

INGREDIENTS

- 1¼ pounds (20 ounces) fresh organic blueberries.
- 2 tablespoons water
- ¼ cup date sugar (or any dry sweetener)
- ½ teaspoon lemon zest
- 1 teaspoon lemon juice

INSTRUCTIONS

- In a medium pot, add 16 ounces of blueberries, along with the water, date sugar, lemon zest and lemon juice. Stir to combine.
- Bring to a boil and reduce to simmer. Simmer until the berries pop.
- Remove from heat and add the other 4 ounces of blueberries and stir. Allow to cool. It will thicken as it cools.

Fluffy Whole Grain Pancakes

INGREDIENTS

- 1 cup unsweetened plant milk
- 1 tablespoon apple cider vinegar
- 1 ¼ cups whole wheat pastry flour (or any flour)
- 1 teaspoon baking powder
- ¼ teaspoon baking soda
- ¼ teaspoon salt
- 2 tablespoons aquafaba
- 2 tablespoons date sugar (or any dry sweetener)
- 1 teaspoon vanilla extract

INSTRUCTIONS

- Combine milk and vinegar in a small measuring cup and set aside to thicken for 10 minutes.
- Combine the flour, baking powder, baking soda, and 1 tablespoon date sugar and salt in a large bowl. Whisk to combine. Add the other tablespoon of date sugar and whisk again.
- Combine the flour mixture with the plant milk. Don't overmix.
- Heat a large griddle over medium heat, about 325°. Add ⅓ cup portions of the batter and cook until bubbles form on top of the pancakes. Flip over and cook for another minute. Serve with fresh fruit and date syrup.

Oatmeal Pancakes

INGREDIENTS

- 2 cups rolled oats
- 1 ½ cups almond milk (or any plant milk)
- 1 tablespoon apple cider vinegar
- 2 tablespoons Kite Hill plain almond yogurt or Forager Unsweetened Cashew Yogurt
- 2 teaspoons vanilla extract
- 2 teaspoons baking powder
- ½ teaspoon baking soda

INSTRUCTIONS

- Place all ingredients in a blender and blend until completely smooth. Heat a flat griddle to 350°
- Ladle batter onto griddle, approximately ¼ cup, and cook until bubbles appear. Flip and cook for another minute.
- Variations: Add chocolate chips, blueberries, bananas or any fruit to the batter.

Nut & Grain Pancakes

INGREDIENTS

- 1 1/2 cups whole-wheat pastry flour or combination of whole-wheat pastry flour and oat flour (3/4 cup each)
- 1 1/2 teaspoons baking powder
- 1/2 teaspoon baking soda
- 1/4 cup finely chopped walnuts
- 1 1/2 cups almond milk
- 2 teaspoons apple cider vinegar
- 2 tablespoons turbinado sugar or date sugar
- 1 teaspoon vanilla extract
- 2 tablespoons ground flax seeds mixed with 6 tablespoons of water (Let it sit for a few minutes.)

INSTRUCTIONS

- In a large bowl, whisk together the flours, baking powder, baking soda and walnuts.
- In another bowl, combine the almond milk and apple cider vinegar and let it sit for 5 minutes. Add the flaxseed mixture, sugar and vanilla. Mix well.
- Add the wet ingredients to the dry ingredients and combine until everything is just mixed together. It may be a little lumpy.
- Heat a non-stick griddle to 350°. Measure out ¼ cup or more and pour on the hot griddle. Cook until a lot of bubbles appear on top and the pancake is golden brown. Flip over and cook the other side as well.
- Top with maple syrup, chopped walnuts, and homemade granola.

This is my copycat recipe for IHOP Harvest Nut & Grain Pancakes

Pancake & Waffle Toppings

TOPPINGS

- Fruits: sliced bananas, chopped pineapple, blueberries, blackberries, sliced strawberries, chopped apples
- Nuts & Seeds: chopped walnuts, pecans, almonds, cashews, hazelnuts, pumpkin seeds, sunflower seeds
- Spices: cinnamon, maple cinnamon sprinkle, etc.
- Kite Hill cream cheese
- Nut Butters: almond, peanut, or cashew
- Maple syrup, date syrup, brown rice syrup
- Chocolate chips

For a fun brunch activity, set up a griddle station and/or a waffle station. Make the batters ahead of time. Show guests how to make their own pancakes and waffles. Have a sign with suggestions. Set up a toppings bar with the following:

Post a sign with recipe ideas such as:

- *Banana Nut*
- *Chocolate Chip*
- *Apple Cinnamon + yogurt & chopped apples*
- *Blueberry Almond*
- *Tropical Waffle with coconut + cashews, topped with pineapple*
- *Hippie Waffle with granola, dried fruit & sunflower seeds*

Baked Goods

Pumpkin Bread with Miso Glaze & Cashew Frosting

Walnut Crusted French Toast

INGREDIENTS

- 4 slices whole grain bread of your choice (My favorite is Heartland bread from Whole Foods or Dave's 21 Grain Bread.)
- 1 cup old fashioned oats (rolled) or brown rice cereal (I used Nature's Path)
- 1 cup walnuts (pecans, almonds, or any nuts)
- 1 teaspoon cinnamon
- 1 tablespoon organic sugar, date sugar, coconut sugar or omit sugar
- Soaking liquid
- 1 cup almond milk
- 1 teaspoon vanilla
- 4 tablespoons applesauce
- 2 tablespoon ground flax seed meal
- 1 tablespoon dry sweetener (unrefined sugar) (optional) maple syrup & fresh diced apple for serving

INSTRUCTIONS

- Preheat oven to 400°
- Place the oats or cereal, nuts, cinnamon and sugar in a food processor and process it until it looks like breadcrumbs. Pour crumbs into a shallow container.
- Place the ingredients for the soaking liquid in a shallow container and mix well. Allow it to sit for 10 minutes for the flax seed to expand. Cut the bread in halves so there are more crispy edges. Dip the bread in the soaking liquid and then place it in the crumbs. Cover it completely with the crumbs. Place the crumb coated bread on a parchment lined baking sheet.
- Bake at 400° degrees for 10 minutes. Turn and bake for 10 more minutes. Serve with maple syrup and fresh fruit, such as cubed apples.

This is the dish to make for Mother's Day, Father's Day or when you want to surprise your significant other with a special breakfast. It's easy to make, looks fancy, and has a wonderful nutty, crunchy texture.

Almond Joy Baked Oatmeal

INGREDIENTS

- 2 cups rolled oats
- 1 T ground flax seeds
- 1 tsp baking powder
- ½ tsp sea salt
- 1 ½ cups almond milk
- 2 teaspoons vanilla extract
- ½ cup maple syrup
- ⅓ cup almond butter
- ½ cup unsweetened shredded coconut
- ⅓ cup chopped roasted almonds
- ½ cup vegan chocolate chips

INSTRUCTIONS

- Preheat oven to 350°
- Mix dry ingredients together in a large bowl. Mix wet ingredients together in a separate bowl.
- Combine them and mix well.
- Place in a 9-inch baking dish and bake at 350° for 35 minutes.
- Top with melted dark chocolate.

Baked Oatmeal with Apples

INGREDIENTS

- 8 servings
- 3 cups rolled oats
- 1 teaspoon baking powder
- ¼ teaspoon kosher salt
- 1 teaspoon cinnamon
- ¾ cup applesauce
- ¼ cup maple or date syrup
- 2 ½ cups plant milk (soy or almond)
- 1 teaspoon vanilla extract
- 1 large apple, chopped
- ⅓ cup raisins
- ⅓ cup chopped nuts (walnuts or almonds)
- 1 tablespoon ground flax seeds
- 3 tablespoon water

INSTRUCTIONS

- Preheat oven to 350°
- Line a 9-inch square pan with parchment paper or use a non-stick USA pan.
- Mix the flax seeds with 1 tablespoon of water in a small bowl and set aside.
- In a large bowl, mix the oats, and the baking powder, salt, and cinnamon.
- In another bowl, mix the applesauce, maple syrup and vanilla extract.
- Combine the dry and wet ingredients. Add the flax mixture. Add the apples, raisins and nuts.
- Pour into the baking pan and bake for 30 minutes or until the edges are lightly brown. It may take up to 35 minutes.

Baked Oatmeal for One

INGREDIENTS

- ½ cup rolled oats
- ½ cup nondairy milk
- 1 tablespoon date syrup
- ½ banana
- ½ teaspoon baking powder
- Pinch of kosher salt
- ½ teaspoon Fresh Jax maple cinnamon topping

INSTRUCTIONS

- Preheat oven to 350°
- Blend in blender or mix by hand
- Place in bowl and add 2 tablespoons dark chocolate chips or any fruit, such as fresh blueberries and 1 tablespoon chopped walnuts or any nuts, mix
- Place in a single serving ramekin and bake at 350° for 30 minutes.

Spelt Banana Bread

INGREDIENTS
- 1 cup spelt flour
- ¾ cup white whole wheat flour (or whole wheat pastry flour)
- ½ cup turbinado sugar (or date sugar)
- ¼ cup unrefined cane sugar (or date sugar)
- 2 ½ teaspoons baking powder
- ¼ teaspoon baking soda
- ¼ teaspoon salt
- 1 teaspoon cinnamon
- 1 tablespoon pumpkin seed protein powder
- 1 cup mashed ripe banana
- 4 tablespoons plant yogurt (Oil free)
- ½ cup soy milk
- ¼ cup apple butter
- ¼ cup almond butter
- 2 tablespoons aquafaba (liquid from canned chickpeas)
- 2 tablespoons maple or date syrup
- 1 cup finely chopped walnuts or pecans
- ½ cup dried cranberries or raisins (or dark chocolate chips)
- Extra walnuts or pecans for garnish

INSTRUCTIONS

- Line a 9x5 loaf pan with parchment paper or use a non-stick USA Pan. Preheat the oven to 360°.
- Combine the flours, sugars, baking powder, baking soda, salt, cinnamon, pumpkin seed protein powder in a large bowl. Mix well with a whisk.
- Directly add mashed bananas, soy milk, yogurt, apple butter, almond butter, and maple syrup. Mix until well combined.
- Place mixture in lined baking pan and top with extra nuts, if desired. Bake for 50 minutes or until toothpick inserted in center comes out almost clean. Cool for 20 minutes before removing from the pan. Cool completely. Keep at room temperature the first day, then it keeps in the refrigerator for 5 days.

If using a muffin tin, bake at 400° for 15 minutes, reduce temperature to 350° and bake for 6-7 more minutes or until toothpick comes out clean.

*Use **Miso Glaze** & **Cashew Frosting** recipe to finish it off. Add 2 teaspoons of the miso glaze to the cashew frosting and taste it. Add more miso glaze until you can taste it, but you don't have to add all of it or the frosting will be too strong. The consistency should be thick. Spoon miso glaze on cooled banana bread.*

Cashew Frosting

INGREDIENTS
- 1 cup raw cashews soaked in water for 30 minutes or longer
- 4 tablespoons almond or soy milk
- 2 tablespoons maple syrup

INSTRUCTIONS
- Drain the cashews and place in a high-speed blender with plant milk and maple syrup. Blend until smooth.
- Add a little more plant milk only if needed to blend the cashews. This mixture should be thick. Scrape down the sides of the blender frequently.

Miso Glaze

INGREDIENTS
- 3 tablespoons white miso paste
- ¼ cup turbinado sugar
- 2-3 tablespoons water

INSTRUCTIONS
- Mix the miso paste with the water to create a smooth mixture. Add the mixture to a small pot along with the turbinado sugar.
- Cook mixture on medium low heat and whisk until it's smooth, about 5 minutes. Remove from heat and set aside.

Pumpkin Bread with Miso Glaze

INGREDIENTS

- 1 cup spelt flour
- ¾ cup white whole wheat flour (or whole wheat pastry flour)
- ½ cup turbinado sugar (or date sugar)
- ¼ cup unrefined cane sugar (or date sugar)
- 2 ½ teaspoons baking powder
- ¼ teaspoon baking soda
- ¼ teaspoon salt
- 2 teaspoons pumpkin pie spice
- 1 tablespoon pumpkin seed protein powder
- 1 cup pumpkin puree
- 4 tablespoons almond milk yogurt (Kite Hill plain almond yogurt) or Forager Unsweetened Cashew Yogurt
- ½ cup soy milk
- 2 tablespoons maple syrup (or date syrup)
- Raw pumpkin seeds for garnish
- Variations: Add ¼ cup chopped walnuts or pecans
- Add ¼ cup chocolate chips
- Add ¼ cup cranberries, raisins, or other dried fruit

You could also use all white whole wheat flour or all whole wheat pastry flour.

INSTRUCTIONS

- Line a 9 by 5 loaf pan with parchment paper or use a non-stick USA Pan. Preheat the oven to 360°.
- Combine the flours, sugars, baking powder, baking soda, salt, pumpkin pie spice and pumpkin seed protein powder in a large bowl. Mix well with a whisk.
- Directly add the pumpkin puree, soy milk, yogurt, and maple syrup. Mix until well combined.
- Place mixture in lined baking pan and sprinkle with pumpkin seeds. Bake for 50 minutes or until toothpick inserted in center comes out almost clean. Cool for 20 minutes before removing from the pan. Cool completely. Keep at room temperature the first day, then it keeps in the refrigerator for 5 days.
- If using a muffin tin, bake at 400° for 15 minutes, reduce temperature to 350° and bake for 6-7 more minutes or until toothpick comes out clean.

*Use **Miso Glaze** & **Cashew Frosting** recipe to finish it off. Add 2 teaspoons of the miso glaze to the cashew frosting and taste it. Add more miso glaze until you can taste it, but you don't have to add all of it or the frosting will be too strong. The consistency should be thick. Spoon miso glaze on cooled pumpkin bread and top with more pumpkin seeds.*

My Favorite Granola

INGREDIENTS

- 6 cups rolled oats
- 2 cups chopped nuts and seeds (I used roasted unsalted cashews, pecans, walnuts, and sunflower seeds.) other options are almonds, sesame seeds, pumpkin seeds
- 1 cup organic unsweetened coconut flakes
- 1 teaspoon cinnamon
- ½ teaspoon salt
- ½ cup maple syrup
- ½ cup organic creamy peanut butter
- Mix the maple syrup with the peanut butter and melt in the microwave for 30 seconds.
- 1 ½ cups dried cranberries (could also use any dried fruit)

INSTRUCTIONS

- Preheat oven to 325°
- Combine everything but the dried fruit. Bake on 2 extra-large parchment lined baking sheets for 25-30 minutes, stirring a couple times to keep edges from burning. Cool slightly and add the dried fruit.
- Other variations: Add dark chocolate chips (vegan) instead of fruit. Add 2 tablespoons of cacao powder before baking. Add ginger, matcha tea, pumpkin pie spice, goji berries, sesame seeds, or citrus zest

HAWAIIAN VERSION

- Use ½ cup cashew butter instead of peanut butter
- Use 1 ½ cup tropical dried fruit such as pineapple and mangos instead of cranberries
- Valrhona passion fruit feves (½ cup) cut up (These are a vegan substitute for white chocolate.)
- Same as above. Add the dried fruit and passion fruit feves after the granola has cooled.

Orange Ginger Almond Chocolate Oat Muffins

INGREDIENTS

- ½ cup almond milk
- 1 teaspoon apple cider vinegar
- 3 bananas or 1 cup mashed bananas
- ¾ cup unsweetened applesauce
- ¼ cup any nut butter (almond or peanut—no sugar added oil type)
- 1 teaspoon vanilla
- 2 ¼ cups rolled oats
- ¼ teaspoon salt
- 2 teaspoons baking powder
- ½ teaspoon baking soda
- Optional sweetener: 3-4 chopped dates, ¼ cup dry sweetener, or ½ cup maple syrup
- ½ cup fresh orange pieces
- ¼ cup chopped almonds
- 2 tablespoons candied ginger
- ½ cup dark chocolate chips

INSTRUCTIONS

- Preheat oven to 350°
- Place the plant milk in a measuring cup and add the teaspoon of apple cider vinegar. Add the mashed bananas, applesauce, almond butter and vanilla to the blender. Add ¼ cup dry sweetener or date or maple syrup, if using, or any dry sweetener or add a couple chopped dates. Blend until smooth.
- In a bowl, mix the oats, salt, baking powder and baking soda together. Add to the blender and blend until smooth. Place the mixture in a bowl and add the orange pieces, ginger, and chocolate chips. Divide the mixture evenly in a 12-compartment muffin pan. If you have a non-stick muffin tin, (USA Pans) add directly to the pan. Otherwise, use muffin/cupcake liners.
- Bake for 20 minutes, check with a toothpick for doneness. If a toothpick comes out clean, they're done.
- Use ½ cup any fresh or dried fruit, ¼ cup chopped nuts, or ½ cup vegan dark chocolate disks or chips

Oatmeal Nut Butter Balls

INGREDIENTS
- 2 cups rolled oats
- ¼ cup oat flour
- ½ cup seeds (hemp, sunflower, flax, pumpkin) I used a combination of hemp, sunflower, pumpkin and flax seeds.
- 1 cup nut butter (peanut or almond) (may need to use a little more if mixture is too dry)
- ⅓ cup syrup (maple, date, brown rice) may need to use a little more if mixture is too dry
- 1 teaspoon vanilla extract
- 4 ounces vegan mini dark chocolate chips (I used El Rey 61% Mijao dark chocolate disks)
- ¼ teaspoon kosher salt
- ½ cup unsweetened coconut flakes (optional)

INSTRUCTIONS

- If you don't want chocolate use ¼ cup dried fruit (raisins or cranberries) and ¼ teaspoon cinnamon
- Place the oats, oat flour, salt and seeds on a baking sheet and bake for 15 minutes in a 300-degree oven.
- Place baked oat mixture in a large bowl.
- Warm the nut butter slightly in the microwave for 30 seconds at 40% power.
- Add the maple syrup (or other syrup) and vanilla to the warm peanut butter and mix well.
- Add to the oat mixture and stir together.
- Add the chocolate chips. Mix well and form into balls.
- Place the balls on a parchment lined baking sheet and chill until firm.
- This recipe made about 30 balls. They can also be frozen.
- Other options include raisins instead of chocolate chips (or cranberries), ¼ teaspoon cinnamon, chopped peanuts or almonds can be added. If mixture is too dry, add small amounts of peanut butter and maple syrup, just enough to hold mixture together.

Oatmeal & Fruit Muffins

INGREDIENTS

- Plant based milk (½ cup) I used almond milk
- 1 teaspoon apple cider vinegar
- 3 bananas or 1 cup mashed bananas
- ¾ cup unsweetened applesauce
- ¼ cup any nut butter (almond or peanut—no sugar added oil type)
- 1 teaspoon vanilla
- 2 ¼ cups rolled oats
- ¼ teaspoon salt
- 2 teaspoons baking powder
- ½ teaspoon baking soda
- Optional sweetener: 3-4 chopped dates, ¼ cup dry sweetener or date syrup
- ½ cup dried fruit, ¼ cup chopped nuts, or ½ cup vegan dark chocolate disks or chips

INSTRUCTIONS

- Preheat oven to 350°
- Non-stick muffin tin for 12 muffins or liners if your muffin tin sticks.
- Place the plant milk in a measuring cup and add the teaspoon of apple cider vinegar. Add the mashed bananas, applesauce, almond butter, and vanilla to the blender. Add ¼ cup coconut sugar, if using, or any dry sweetener or add a couple chopped dates instead of dried sweetener. Blend until smooth.
- In a bowl, mix the oats, salt, baking powder and baking soda together. Add to the blender and blend until smooth.
- Place the mixture in a bowl and add the chocolate chips or dried fruit and nuts.
- Divide the mixture evenly in the 12 compartments. If you have a non-stick muffin tin, (USA Pans) add directly to the pan. Otherwise, use muffin/cupcake liners.
- Bake for 20 minutes, check with a toothpick for doneness. If toothpick comes out clean, they're done.

Double Chocolate Oatmeal Muffins: (pictured)

- Add 1 tablespoon cacao powder to the muffin batter, along with chocolate chips and nuts.

Cinnamon Rolls

These Cinnamon Rolls are oil-free, made with whole wheat pastry flour, unsweetened applesauce, dried fruit and optional walnuts. They can be glazed or left plain, but in either version they are really special.

INGREDIENTS

- ¾ cup non-dairy milk (I used almond milk.)
- 1 packet instant yeast. (Brand is Red Star Platinum Instant Yeast)
- 3 cups whole wheat pastry flour plus more for the kneading and rolling
- 1 tablespoon baking powder
- ¼ cup cane sugar, date sugar, or any dry sweetener
- 1 teaspoon cinnamon
- ¼ teaspoon salt
- 6 tablespoons unsweetened applesauce

FILLING

- 1 teaspoon cinnamon
- 2 tablespoons unsweetened applesauce
- 4 tablespoons turbinado or brown sugar (or any dry sweetener)
- 2 tablespoons raisins
- ¼ cup chopped walnuts

GLAZE

- 1 cup organic cane confectioner's sugar
- 2 tablespoons or more almond milk

INSTRUCTIONS

- Preheat oven to 350°
- Line a 9-inch cake pan with parchment paper.
- Gently warm 3/4 cup non-dairy milk (almond milk), in a pan to about 110 degrees.
- Sprinkle the yeast over the warmed milk and let it dissolve, about 5 minutes.
- Combine 3 cups of whole-wheat pastry flour, ¼ cup dry sweetener, baking powder, 1 teaspoon cinnamon and ¼ teaspoon salt in a large bowl. Mix well with a whisk. Add 6 tablespoons applesauce and yeast mixture, stirring to combine.
- Sprinkle a large cutting board or countertop with a handful of four and knead the dough 15-20 times, or until it comes together in a soft ball that can be rolled out. Add flour as necessary to keep it from sticking.
- Using a floured rolling pin, roll out the dough into a large 12"x10" rectangle. Set aside.

FILLING

- Combine cinnamon, unsweetened applesauce, turbinado sugar and raisins in a small bowl.
- Spread the filling on the dough rectangle, leaving a 1-inch border on all sides.
- Sprinkle with the walnuts. Roll it tightly, using a dough scraper to keep the dough from sticker to the board, if needed.
- Using a sharp knife, cut into equal pieces, approximately 7. Place the cut pieces in the cake pan and bake for 25 minutes or until the internal temperature is 190°

GLAZE

- Sift the confectioner's sugar and place it in a medium bowl. Add the almond milk, a little at a time until the glaze is the right thickness and can be spooned on top of the cinnamon rolls.
- Allow the rolls to cool before glazing them.

Apple Crisp

INGREDIENTS

- 3 pounds apples, peeled, cored, and sliced into ½ slices, approximately 6-7 cups (Gala is what I used, but you can use Pink Lady, Honeycrisp or others.)
- 6 ounces unsweetened apple juice
- 2 teaspoons freshly squeezed lemon juice
- 2 teaspoons vanilla extract
- 2 teaspoons cinnamon
- 2 teaspoons arrowroot powder (or cornstarch)
- ¼ teaspoon nutmeg
- ¼ teaspoon kosher salt or sea salt
- 1 cup old-fashioned (whole) oats
- ¼ cup flour (whole wheat, almond, gluten free)
- 3 tablespoon unrefined sugar or choice (coconut, turbinado, maple)
- 2 tablespoon real maple syrup or date syrup (or any syrup you like)
- ½ cup chopped walnuts
- ½ cup chopped dates

INSTRUCTIONS

- Preheat the oven to 350°.
- In a large bowl, combine the apples, juice, lemon juice, vanilla, cinnamon, arrowroot, nutmeg, and salt. Mix together well and place in a 13x9 baking dish.
- In a separate bowl, combine the oatmeal, flour, sugar, syrup and a pinch of salt. Mix well.
- Spread the mixture over the apples. Add the walnuts and dates.
- Cover the baking dish with foil and bake covered for 45 minutes. Remove foil and bake for an additional 10 minutes or until it's golden brown. Serve hot, warm or cold.
- Substitute pears, plums, peaches, or other similar fruit for the apples and adjust the cooking time for softer fruit, probably to 30-35 minutes covered.

This is a comforting dish that the entire family will love. The natural sweetness from the apples and the crunchy nuts cooked together with the oats create a dessert feel, however I've enjoyed this for breakfast too!

Oatmeal Breakfast Cookies

INGREDIENTS

- 1 ½ cups oat flour (blend whole oats in Vitamix)
- ½ cup whole oats
- ½ cup maple syrup (or date syrup or combo of both)
- ½ cup almond butter or any nut butter
- 1 tablespoon ground flax seeds (optional)
- ½ cup unsweetened coconut flakes (optional)
- 2 teaspoons vanilla powder (or extract)
- 1 tablespoon pumpkin seed protein powder
- ½ cup any dried fruit such as raisins, cranberries, cherries, blueberries or ½ cup vegan chocolate chips
- ½ cup chopped nuts (almonds, walnuts, pecans, pistachios)

INSTRUCTIONS

- Preheat oven to 350°
- Combine all ingredients in a bowl and form a dough.
- Scoop the dough into 2 tablespoon size balls and place them on a parchment lined baking sheet.
- Flatten the balls with your hand.
- Bake for 10 minutes or until lightly brown on the edges.

Fruit & Nut Bars

INGREDIENTS

- 1 cup rolled (old-fashioned) oats 1 cup oat flour
- 1 teaspoon cinnamon
- 1 teaspoon baking powder
- ¼ teaspoon salt
- 2 ripe bananas, mashed or ½ cup apple butter or applesauce
- ½ cup soy milk
- 1-2 tablespoons maple or date syrup

Options:

2 cups fresh strawberries, sliced into quarters or blueberries, raspberries, blackberries, or chopped dates (5 or 6), dried cranberries or other dried fruit (½ cup), ⅓ cup chopped nuts (walnuts, almonds, pecans), 1-2 tablespoons flax, chia, hemp seeds, ¼ cup coconut flakes

INSTRUCTIONS

- Preheat the oven to 350°
- Line an 8-inch square baking dish with 2 pieces of parchment paper. Combine the oatmeal, oat flour, cinnamon, baking powder and salt in a medium size bowl.
- In a separate bowl, mash the banana and add the soy milk and syrup. If using apple butter or applesauce, mix that with the soy milk and syrup.
- Combine the dry ingredients with the wet ingredients. Place ⅔ of the batter in the lined baking dish. Sprinkle the fruit or dates on top. Spoon the rest of the batter on top. Sprinkle with nuts and seeds, and more cinnamon, if desired.
- Bake for 18-20 minutes. Cool on the cooling rack for 10 minutes and slice into bars. Keeps for 3-4 days in a sealed container at room temperature.

These are so handy to have when you're going to be away from home and need something to eat when everyone around you is snacking on processed food. These bars keep well for a few days but don't freeze well, so make a small batch and eat them all up.

Chocolate Peanut Butter Date Bars

INGREDIENTS

No Bake Cookie Layer

- ¾ cup peanut butter
- ¼ cup maple or date syrup
- 1 ½ teaspoons vanilla extract
- ¼ teaspoon kosher salt
- 1 cup almond flour
- 1 ½ cups cashew flour (or almond)
- 2 tablespoons pumpkin seed protein powder
- 1 cup chopped dark chocolate or vegan chocolate chips

- **Date Layer**
- 1 ½ cups walnuts (or any nuts you prefer)
- 2 tablespoons cacao powder
- ¼ teaspoon kosher salt or sea salt
- 10 dates (pits removed)
- 2 tablespoons water
- 2 tablespoons finely chopped walnuts
- Maldon Sea Salt for topping

INSTRUCTIONS
No Bake Cookie Layer

- Mix the peanut butter, maple syrup, vanilla, and salt together in a large bowl, until well combined. Fold in the chopped chocolate or chocolate chips.
- Press into a 9-inch square pan lined with parchment paper. Place the pan in the freezer.

Date Layer

- Place the walnuts, cacao powder, and salt in a food processor and process until the nuts are finely chopped. Add the dates and continue to process. If the mixture gets stuck, add the water. Continue to process the mixture until it's smooth.
- Spread it onto the crust layer. Sprinkle with the finely chopped nuts and Maldon Sea Salt. Freeze for another 30 minutes or longer. Remove from the pan and cut into bars. They can be stored in the freezer or refrigerator.

Savory

Biscuits, Sausage, Hatch Grits, & Breakfast Tofu

Vegetable Frittata

INGREDIENTS

- 1 cup moong dal (split mung beans)
- ½ teaspoon kosher salt
- ½ teaspoon kala namak (black salt)
- ¼ teaspoon garlic powder
- ¼ teaspoon onion powder
- ¼ teaspoon ground turmeric
- 1 cup cashew milk
- 3 cremini mushrooms, washed, dried and sliced thin
- ¼ of a large orange or red bell pepper, sliced into matchstick pieces
- ¼ cup sliced red onion
- ¼ cup thinly sliced zucchini
- 1 cup baby spinach or mixed greens
- 1 clove garlic • ½ teaspoon salt
- 1 teaspoon fresh thyme, minced
- 1 teaspoon fresh rosemary, minced
- Pinch of cayenne pepper
- Freshly ground black pepper
- 1 tablespoon nutritional yeast (optional)
- ½ cup Crispy Tofu Cubes (optional)

INSTRUCTIONS

- Wash and soak the split mung beans in water to cover by 3 inches, overnight. Drain well and add to a blender. Add the salt, kala namak, garlic and onion powder, black pepper, and turmeric. Add 1 cup cashew milk. Blend for a minute, then let it rest and blend for another minute. It should be smooth and fluffy. To make it fluffier, add 1 teaspoon baking powder.
- To cook the frittata, heat a 12-inch non-stick skillet over medium high heat.
- To make plain omelets without vegetables such as a folded egg for a sandwich, add ¼ cup or more of the batter to the skillet. Cover the skillet with a lid and cook for a couple minutes. Flip it over and cook for another minute. Fold it into a square or serve it as a plain omelet

For the Vegetable Frittata:

- Add the mushrooms to the skillet and cook for 3-4 minutes. Add the onions, zucchini, bell pepper and jalapeno peppers. Add the garlic, salt and herbs. Cook for 2-3 minutes. Add a handful of spinach or mixed greens.
- Separate the vegetables into 4 sections. Add batter to each section so you have 4 portions. This will make them easier to turn over. Place the lid on the skillet and cook for 2-3 minutes. Flip them over and cook for a couple more minutes.
- The batter will keep in the refrigerator for 2 days. It can also be used to make French toast, but omit the salt.

Biscuits & Sausage Gravy

INGREDIENTS

Biscuits

- 2 cups all-purpose (unbleached) flour or 2 cups white whole wheat flour or whole wheat pastry flour
- 1 tablespoon baking powder
- ½ teaspoon salt

Cashew Cream

- 2/3 cup raw cashews, soaked in water for 30 minutes
- 1 ¼ cups cold water

Sausage Gravy

- 2-3 sausage patties (made in recipe on next page) • 2 cups cashew milk (2 cups raw cashews, soaked for at least 30 minutes, blend, add 4 cups water, blend until smooth)
- ¼ cup whole wheat pastry flour or brown rice flour
- ½ cup water
- Salt and pepper to taste
- Red pepper flakes

INSTRUCTIONS

Biscuits

- Preheat oven to 475°
- Make the cashew cream in a blender by draining the soaked cashews well. Add 1 ¼ cup water to the cashews and blend until smooth and creamy.
- In a large bowl, whisk the flour, baking powder and salt. Add the cashew cream a little at a time until a dough forms. Place the mixture on a floured surface and sprinkle it with flour as needed to form dough, using a bench scraper to move it around gently. Form the dough into a circle, about 8-9 inches in diameter and ½ inch thick. Cut out biscuits with a biscuit cutter and place on a parchment lined baking sheet. Bake for 10-12 minutes.

Sausage Gravy

- Heat the cashew milk in a medium size pot. Add the flour to the ½ cup water in a small bowl and mix well. Add the flour mixture to the cashew milk and cook until the mixture is bubbling and thickened, about 3-5 minutes.
- Add salt, freshly ground black pepper and red pepper flakes, if desired. Crumble in some plant-based sausage.

WFPB Sausage

INGREDIENTS

- 2 ½ cups quick oats (or whole oats processed in food processor)
- ½ cup walnuts, ground in food processor
- 3 tablespoons ground flax seeds
- ½ cup cooked brown rice
- 2 tablespoons nutritional yeast
- ½ tablespoon onion powder
- ½ tablespoon garlic powder• 1 teaspoon paprika
- 1 teaspoon oregano
- ½ teaspoon black pepper
- ½ teaspoon ground sage
- ½ teaspoon ground fennel
- ½ teaspoon dried thyme
- ½ teaspoon cumin
- ½ teaspoon kosher salt
- Pinch cayenne pepper
- Pinch red pepper flakes
- 1 tablespoon maple syrup
- ½ teaspoon liquid smoke
- 1 cup vegetable stock
- 1 cup water
- 2 tablespoons low-sodium soy sauce

INSTRUCTIONS

- Combine oats, walnuts, ground flax seeds, brown rice, nutritional yeast, and all spices in a large bowl.
- In a small saucepan add the vegetable stock, water, maple syrup, liquid smoke and low-sodium soy sauce. Simmer briefly. Add the warm liquid to the oat mixture and mix well. Let the mixture sit for about 10 minutes to firm up.
- Using a 3 tablespoons size cookie scoop, measure out 16 portions on two parchment lined baking sheets. Press into circles. Bake at 350° for 15 minutes. Turn the patties over and bake for 5 more minutes.

Breakfast Tofu

INGREDIENTS

- 1 block extra firm tofu (14 ounces)
- ¼ cup low sodium soy sauce
- 2 tablespoons maple syrup
- 1 tablespoon nutritional yeast (optional)
- 1 teaspoon liquid smoke
- 1 teaspoon onion powder
- ½ teaspoon garlic powder
- ½ teaspoon paprika
- Dash cayenne pepper
- Freshly ground black pepper

INSTRUCTIONS

- Pre-heat the oven to 400° or 375° convection setting
- Drain and press tofu by wrapping the tofu in paper towels, a cloth, and placing a cutting board on top. Place a couple heavy books on the cutting board. Press the tofu for 15-20 minutes. Cut the tofu into ¼ inch slices, approximately 12 slices. Marinate the tofu for at least 30 minutes or longer.
- Place it on a parchment lined baking sheet and bake for 25-30 minutes at 400°
- You can also use the air fryer at 350° for 5 minutes per side and keep cooking until desired doneness.

Avocado Toast

INGREDIENTS

- Bread of your choice--sourdough, whole grain (no oil)
- 1 avocado
- Sea salt • Red chili flakes
- 1 tablespoon toasted pumpkin seeds
- Maldon sea salt
- Red onion slices or pickled red onion (place onion slices in vinegar for a few minutes)
- Salsa such as salsa verde or red salsa
- Lime juice
- Arugula
- Sesame seeds
- *Everything But the Bagel* Seasoning

INSTRUCTIONS

- Toast the bread. Either slice the avocado or mash it with a fork and add some lime juice and sea salt to it.
- Place the avocado on the toasted bread. Add any of the seasonings, red onion slices, greens, and salsa.

Classic Tofu Scramble

INGREDIENTS

- 1 (14 ounce) block extra firm tofu, drained and wrapped in paper towels (Nasoya or Wildwood Organic Tofu)
- 1 cup chopped yellow onion
- 4 cremini mushrooms, sliced or chopped
- 1-2 Roma tomatoes, chopped (no seeds)
- 3 teaspoons minced fresh garlic
- 1 Serrano chili (omit for not spicy version)
- ¼ cup vegetable stock
- 1 tablespoon fresh lemon juice
- 1 teaspoon turmeric
- Pinch black salt (Kala Namak)
- Or
- 2 tablespoons Fresh Jax Tofu Scramble Seasoning
- 2 scallions, thinly sliced
- ¼ cup fresh cilantro, chopped

INSTRUCTIONS

- In a large skillet over medium high heat, add the onions and saute for 3-5 minutes, until they start to brown lightly.
- Add the mushrooms and stir. Saute until the mushrooms are lightly browned, about 4-5 minutes more.
- Add the chopped tomatoes, garlic and a little vegetable stock. Sauté for a couple more minutes.
- Crumble in the tofu and stir gently. Add the turmeric, black salt, lemon juice and the rest of the vegetable stock.
- Serve with avocado slices, thinly sliced scallions, sliced jalapenos, and chopped fresh cilantro.

Hashbrown Casserole

INGREDIENTS

Cheese Sauce

- 1 cup peeled and diced potatoes (Yukon Gold)
- ¼ cup diced carrots
- ¼ cup diced onions
- 1 cup vegetable broth
- ½ cup raw cashews, soaked in water for at least 30 minutes or longer
- 1 teaspoon lemon juice
- 2 tablespoons Fresh Jax Tofu Scramble Seasoning

OR

- 1-2 tablespoons nutritional yeast (or omit if you don't like the taste)
- 1 teaspoon tamari (low sodium)
- ¼ teaspoon garlic powder
- ¼ teaspoon paprika
- Pinch of cayenne powder

Hash Brown Casserole

- 1 (16 ounce) bag frozen hash browns (oil free such as Trader Joe's or Alexia brand)
- ½ cup diced onions
- ¼ cup diced red bell pepper
- ¾ cup fresh baby spinach, cut into pieces
- 1 cup plant-based cheese sauce
- 1 tablespoon nutritional yeast (optional)
- ½ teaspoon no salt seasoning blend (Trader Joe's 21 Seasoning Salute or Costco No Salt Seasoning or blend of your choice)
- 1 teaspoon paprika
- ¼ cup finely chopped cilantro
- 2 scallions, thinly sliced
- 1 jalapeno pepper or Fresno chili, thinly sliced

INSTRUCTIONS

Cheese Sauce

- Cook the potatoes, carrots, and onions in a medium pot with water to cover. Bring to a boil, reduce to simmer and cook for approximately 20 minutes or until fork tender. Drain well, but keep the cooking liquid.

- Blend the cooked vegetables, spices, tamari, 1 cup of the reserved liquid, soaked cashews, and lemon juice in the blender. If you don't want to use cashews, omit the cashew and use double the amount of carrots and ½ cup more potatoes and another ¼ teaspoon of paprika.

- Remove from the blender and set aside.

Hashbrown Casserole

- In a large skillet over medium high heat, add the onions and bell peppers. Cook for 3-5 minutes, adding a little water or vegetable stock and covering with a lid for a couple more minutes over medium heat.

- Add the cooked vegetables to a large bowl along with the frozen hash browns, cheese sauce, chopped spinach, and seasonings.

- Place in a 9-inch baking dish and bake at 350° for 40-45 minutes or until the top is lightly brown and the potatoes are hot.

- Drizzle more cheese sauce on top along with finely chopped cilantro, scallions, and jalapeno peppers, is desired. Serve with additional cheese sauce.

Tofu Bacon

INGREDIENTS

- 1 (14 ounce) block of extra firm tofu, drained and pressed, and sliced thin
- ½ cup low sodium soy sauce
- 1 tablespoon tomato paste
- 1 tablespoon vegan Worcestershire sauce
- 1 tablespoon maple syrup
- 1 tablespoon liquid smoke

INSTRUCTIONS

- Press tofu by draining it well. Wrap it in a clean cloth towel and place it under a cutting board. Set a heavy book on top and press the tofu for 20 minutes.
- Mix marinade ingredients together in a small bowl. Add sliced tofu to the marinade. Marinate for a couple hours or overnight.
- Cook the slices in a skillet or on a griddle over medium high heat until browned and crispy.

Creamy Grits

INGREDIENTS

- 1 cup stoneground yellow or white grits
- 3 ½ cups vegetable stock
- ½ cup cashew milk. (Blend ½ cup cashews + ½ cup water)
- ½ cup diced onion
- ¼ cup bell pepper
- 1 clove garlic
- ½ teaspoon onion powder
- ½ teaspoon garlic powder
- Freshly ground black pepper
- 1 cup chopped greens (kale, spinach, chard)

INSTRUCTIONS

- In a medium size pot over medium high heat, cook the onions until they are softened, add a little water as needed. Add the bell peppers. Cover the pan for and cook for 3 minutes to soften the onions and bell peppers.
- Add the vegetable stock and cashew milk and bring it to a boil. With a whisk, slowly add the grits, whisking as you add them.
- Cook over low heat for 20-40 minutes, depending on the grits, it can take up to 40 minutes.
- If you like them spicy, add red pepper flakes.

Crispy, Pan-Fried Potatoes

INGREDIENTS

- 3 medium size russet potatoes, peeled and diced into ½ inch pieces
- ½ cup thinly sliced green bell peppers
- ½ cup thinly sliced sweet yellow onion
- 3 garlic cloves, minced
- ½ teaspoon salt-free seasoning blend such as Trader Joe's 21 Seasoning Salute
- ½ teaspoon salt
- ¼ teaspoon turmeric
- ¼ teaspoon red chili powder
- 2 tablespoons fresh parsley, minced
- ½ teaspoon red pepper flakes

INSTRUCTIONS

- Cook the potatoes first by placing them in a pot with water to barely cover the potatoes. Bring to a boil and reduce to a simmer. Cook until not quite done, about 5 minutes. They should still be a little firm. Drain and set aside.
- Heat a 12-inch skillet over medium high heat. Add the onions and peppers and cook them for minutes. Put a lid on the skillet and cook for a couple more minutes.
- Add the potatoes and spices. Cook on medium low heat for 4 minutes without turning. Turn and cook another 4 minutes, or until they are cooked through.
- Place on a serving platter and sprinkle with the fresh parsley and red pepper flakes.

Savory Steel-Cut Oatmeal

INGREDIENTS

- ½ cup steel cut oats
- 2 cups water
- Pinch of kosher salt
- 2 broccoli florets, chopped (about ¼ cup)
- 2-inch piece yellow summer squash or zucchini, chopped, (about ¼ cup)
- Or ¼ cup fresh green beans, cut into 2-inch pieces
- ¼ cup chopped yellow onion
- 1 garlic clove, minced
- ½ medium tomato, chopped
- ½ jalapeno pepper, minced (optional)
- Or Jimmy Nardello peppers, diced
- 3 tablespoons cooked greens, chopped
- ¼ teaspoon Fresh Jax Vampepper seasoning blend (or a garlic pepper blend)
- ¼ teaspoon Fresh Jax Tofu Scramble seasoning blend (or pinch of nutritional yeast)
- 1 scallion, thinly sliced
- Red pepper flakes

INSTRUCTIONS

Cooking the Steel Cut Oats

- Bring the water to a boil and add the steel cut oats. Reduce to simmer and cook until water is mostly absorbed, about 15 minutes. Keep the oats a little chewy, not over cooked or they get too soft.

Savory Steel Cut Oatmeal

- In a skillet over medium high heat, add the chopped onions and garlic and sauté until lightly browned.
- Add the rest of the vegetables and cook for 3 more minutes. Add a couple tablespoons of water, reduce the heat and cover with a lid. Cook for 2 minutes.
- Add the cooked steel cut oats to the skillet and stir. Add the greens and spices.
- Serve with scallions and red pepper flakes, and some avocado.

This recipe can be made with just about any fresh or leftover vegetable you have on hand.

Breakfast Sandwich with Sausage, Savory Tofu & Cheese Sauce

Sausage

INGREDIENTS

- 3 ½ cups water
- ¼ cup low sodium soy sauce or Bragg's Aminos or Tamari 1/4 cup nutritional yeast
- 1 tablespoon onion powder
- 1 tablespoon dried rosemary
- 1 tablespoon maple syrup
- 2 ½ teaspoons dried sage
- 2 teaspoons dried thyme
- 1/2 teaspoon liquid smoke
- 1/2 teaspoon cayenne pepper
- 3 cups quick-cooking Quick oats
- ½ cup cooked brown rice

INSTRUCTIONS

- Heat oven to 350°. Line two large baking sheets with parchment.
- Combine all ingredients except oats and rice in a medium saucepan. Bring to a boil over high heat. Remove from heat and add oats and rice. Stir to combine. Let it sit for 5 minutes.
- Scoop mixture into 2-inch round balls or larger, depending on how big you want the sausage patties.
- Place balls on a baking sheet and flatten gently with the back of a wet spoon. Bake for 15 minutes and flip over. Bake for 5 more minutes.
- Optional step for darker color: brush or spray with soy sauce for the last 5 minutes of baking time.

Savory Tofu

INGREDIENTS

- 1 (14 ounce) package extra firm organic tofu, drained and pressed, cut into round shapes or sliced into 8 pieces
- 1 tablespoon low sodium soy sauce
- 1 tablespoon vegan Worcestershire sauce
- 1 tablespoons coconut aminos
- 1 tablespoons tahini
- 1 teaspoon garlic powder
- 1 teaspoon onion powder
- ½ teaspoon thyme
- 1 teaspoon paprika
- ¼ teaspoon cayenne
- ¼ teaspoon salt
- ¼ teaspoon black pepper
- 1 teaspoon lemon zest
- 1 tablespoon water
- ¼ teaspoon turmeric
- 1 tablespoon maple syrup
- 1 tablespoon Dijon mustard

INSTRUCTIONS

For Conventional Oven:

- Preheat oven to 375°. Line a baking sheet with parchment paper or silpat.
- Remove the tofu from the package, drain, and rinse with water. Wrap the tofu with paper towels. Place the tofu on a cutting board set on top of a baking sheet and place a second cutting board on top of it. Place a heavy object on top of the cutting boards for approximately 10-15 minutes to press the liquid out of the tofu. Change the paper towels after 5 minutes. Alternately, use a tofu press.
- Cut the tofu into round shapes or 8 slices.
- Mix the soy sauce, Worcestershire sauce, coconut aminos, tahini, water, and spices in a large shallow baking dish. Place the slabs of tofu in the marinade and coat all sides well.
- Place the tofu on parchment or silpat lined baking sheets. Bake for 20 minutes, turn over and bake for 5 more minutes.

Air Fryer Instructions:

- Drain and press tofu as above, cut into desired shapes.
- Place in air fryer at 350° for 5 minutes, turn and cook for 5 more minutes. Watch carefully as the air fryer will overcook tofu very easily. Cook longer at a high heat if you want crispier, darker tofu.
- Brush with a mixture of 1 tablespoon maple syrup mixed with 1 tablespoon of Dijon mustard.

Cheese Sauce

INGREDIENTS

- 1 cup raw cashews, soaked for 1 hour in ½ cup water
- ¼ cup nutritional yeast
- ½ tablespoon white/yellow miso
- 1 teaspoon fresh lemon juice
- ½ cup roasted red bell pepper
- ½ teaspoon smoked paprika
- 1 teaspoon paprika
- 1 teaspoon garlic powder
- 1 teaspoon onion powder

INSTRUCTIONS

- Blend all in a high-speed blender

Crispy Tofu Cubes

INGREDIENTS

- 1 (14 ounce) block tofu, drained and pressed, cut into small cubes
- 1 tablespoon Mighty Sesame Tahini
- 1 tablespoon low sodium soy sauce
- 1 teaspoon seasoning blend of your choice
- 1 teaspoon of Tofu Scramble seasoning
- Light sprinkle of Sriracha salt.

INSTRUCTIONS

- Press tofu by draining it well. Wrap it in a clean cloth towel and place it under a cutting board. Set a heavy book on top and press the tofu for 20 minutes.
- Add all ingredients.
- Air fry on 350° for 5 minutes, turn and air fry for 5 more minutes or until golden brown and a little crispy. If using a regular oven, bake at 375° for 25 minutes or until brown and crispy.

Southwestern + Tex-Mex

Hatch Tofu Scramble on top of Hatch Grits

Breakfast Tacos
+Chipotle Tofu
+Chipotle Aioli
+Guacamole

INGREDIENTS

- 12 tortillas, corn or corn/flour blend (I buy the Sprouts store brand or La Tortilla Factory brand.)
- Shredded lettuce
- Diced tomatoes
- Salsa of your choice

INSTRUCTIONS

- Warm the tortillas on a griddle on in a skillet on medium high heat.
- Add the potatoes, tofu, chipotle aioli, guacamole, lettuce, tomatoes, and any other toppings of your choice.

Chipotle Tofu

INGREDIENTS

- 1 (14 ounce) package extra firm tofu, drained and pressed (Wrap in paper towel/cloth towel)
- ¼ cup maple syrup
- 2 tablespoons adobo sauce (from a can of Chipotle in Adobo)
- 2 tablespoons lime juice
- 1 tablespoon soy sauce
- 1 garlic clove, minced
- 1 teaspoon ground cumin
- 1 teaspoon paprika

INSTRUCTIONS

- Preheat oven to 400°. Use a USA baking sheet or line a baking sheet with parchment paper.
- Cut the tofu block into 8 slices and cut the slices into small cubes.
- Mix the marinade ingredients together in a small bowl. Place the tofu in a glass container and mix well with the marinade ingredients. Marinate for 15-20 minutes.
- Bake on prepared baking sheets for 20 minutes, turn over and bake 20 more minutes.

Chipotle Aioli

INGREDIENTS

- 1 cup raw cashews, soaked for 30 minutes or longer
- 1/3 cup water
- 2 tablespoons adobo sauce (from the Chipotle in Adobo can used for the tofu)
- 2 tablespoons apple cider vinegar or red wine vinegar
- 1/2 teaspoon ground cumin
- ½ teaspoon onion powder
- ½ teaspoon garlic powder
- ½ teaspoon kosher salt

INSTRUCTIONS

- Place all ingredients into a high-speed blender and blend until smooth. Scrape down sides as necessary.

Guacamole

INGREDIENTS

- 2 ripe avocados
- ¼ cup finely chopped cilantro
- 2 tablespoons finely diced red onion
- 1 clove garlic, minced
- Freshly ground sea salt

INSTRUCTIONS

- In a medium size bowl, mash the avocado with a fork. I like to leave it a bit chunky.
- Add the cilantro, lime juice, red onion, garlic and salt. Mix together gently.

Spicy Potatoes

INGREDIENTS

- 2 pounds organic russet potatoes, washed and cut into ½ inch pieces (peels on or off)
- 1 tablespoon cornstarch
- 1 teaspoon cumin
- 1 teaspoon paprika
- ½ teaspoon ancho chili powder
- ½ teaspoon kosher salt
- Pinch freshly ground black pepper
- 2 tablespoons tahini (Mighty Sesame Tahini)

INSTRUCTIONS

- Preheat oven to 400° and prepare a baking sheet with parchment paper or use a non-stick baking sheet.
- Place the potatoes in a pot of boiling water and boil until they are slightly tender, about 5 minutes. They should still have body left to them, so don't over-cook. Drain the potatoes and place them in a bowl.
- Add the cornstarch, spices, and tahini. Stir to coat well.
- Place the potatoes on the baking sheet and bake for 20-25 minutes. You can also use the air fryer and bake at 375° for 5 minutes, turn and cook for 5 more minutes or until crispy and done.

These potatoes can be served inside the tacos and alongside the Frittata. Make extra to serve with the frittata.

Hatch Green Chili Grits

INGREDIENTS

- 1 cup stone ground yellow or white grits (Bob's Red Mill, Homestead Gristmill, Food for the Southern Soul Charleston Grits, but not quick grits)
- 1 cup diced yellow onions
- 2 garlic cloves, minced
- ¼ cup diced Hatch green chiles (canned or from a jar)
- ½ teaspoon Chipotle pepper powder or 1 Chipotle in Adobo, rinsed and chopped
- 4 cups vegetable stock
- 2 teaspoons nutritional yeast (optional)
- Juice of ½ lime
- Salt and pepper to taste
- 1-2 cups mixed greens (kale, chard, spinach)
- Fresh cilantro (¼ cup)
- 2-3 scallions, sliced thinly

INSTRUCTIONS

- In a medium size pot over medium high heat, cook the onions until they are softened, adding a tablespoon of water as needed. Cover the pan and cook for 3 minutes to soften the onions.
- Add the garlic and green chiles and chipotle pepper and cook for 5 minutes with a little stock. Add the rest of the stock and bring it to a boil.
- With a whisk, slowly add the grits, whisking as you add them. Cook over low heat for 20-40 minutes. Some stone-ground grits require 30 minutes or more to cook completely. Stir occasionally.
- When done, add a handful of greens and stir again.
- Top with chopped fresh cilantro and thinly sliced scallions.

Hatch Green Chili Tofu Scramble

INGREDIENTS

- Extra firm tofu, 14-ounce block, drained and wrapped in a towel
- 1 cup onion
- ½ cup cremini mushrooms (baby portobello)
- 3 garlic cloves
- ½ cup chopped Hatch green chiles from canned, drained chiles or a jar
- ½ tsp paprika
- ½ tsp onion powder
- ½ tsp turmeric
- Salt, to taste
- Freshly ground black pepper
- ½ tsp garlic powder
- 2 tablespoons nutritional yeast or 2 tablespoons Fresh Jax Tofu Scramble blend
- ¼ cup cilantro
- ½ tsp soy sauce
- 1 tsp fresh lemon juice
- 1 jalapeño sliced thin

INSTRUCTIONS

- In a 12-inch skillet on medium high heat, add onion and cook for 3-4 minutes until it starts to brown and stick to the pan. Add 2 tablespoons of water.
- Stir and add the garlic and mushrooms. Continue cooking undisturbed for a couple more minutes, allowing the onions and mushrooms to brown and caramelize.
- Stir and add a couple tablespoons of water. Cover and reduce the heat to medium and cook for 6-7 minutes.
- While the onion mixture is cooking, mix together all the spices and nutritional yeast.
- After 6-7 minutes, add the tofu to the skillet by crumbling it with your fingers into the pan in irregular sized pieces.
- Add all the spices and the Hatch green chiles. Mix gently. Add the cilantro, soy sauce, and lemon juice.
- Serve with the grits. I like to put a mound of grits on the plate and place the tofu scramble on top of the grits.

Austin Breakfast Tacos + Tofu Sausage

INGREDIENTS

- 6 corn tortillas (or corn/flour blend tortillas with no oil)
- Salsa with no salt and no oil
- Avocado slices
- Chopped cilantro
- Sliced scallions
- Sliced jalapeno peppers
- Tofu Sausage (recipe below)

Tofu Sausage

1 (14 ounce) package extra firm tofu, drained and pressed (Use a tofu press or wrap the tofu in cotton towel and place a cutting board on top of it with a heavy object on top of the board. I use a large cookbook.)

Marinade Ingredients

- 3 tablespoons low sodium soy sauce (or coconut aminos)
- 1 tablespoon tahini
- 1 teaspoon chili powder
- 2 teaspoons ground cumin seeds
- ½ teaspoon garlic powder
- ½ cup finely chopped walnuts • ½ cup finely chopped red onions • 2 tablespoons nutritional yeast (I like Sari brand.)

A traditional Japanese breakfast consists of one soup and three dishes, just like any typical meal. Misoshiru soup, rice, seaweed, umeboshi (pickled plums), and Natto, fermented soybeans are popular breakfast foods, along with grilled fish and eggs. Of course, with the plant-based way of eating, we can substitute baked tofu for fish, and tofu scramble for the eggs or eat any savory food we enjoy for breakfast. An additional dish of seasonal fruit or vegetables can also be added. In my photo of the Japanese breakfast, I added sliced cucumbers from my garden.

Japanese Breakfast

Miso Soup

INGREDIENTS

- 5 cups water or homemade vegetable broth
- 1 teaspoon Takii (mushroom stock powder) or ground dried shiitake mushrooms
- 1 cup vegetables: Choose one or more-- ½ cup thinly sliced mushrooms, ½ cup corn, ½ cup sliced snow peas, ½ cup julienne carrots, ½ cup cubed sweet or white potatoes, ½ cup chopped onions, ½ cup sliced green beans, ½ cup peas, ½ cup diced zucchini, ½ cup sliced cabbage
- 1 tablespoon dried wakame seaweed, rehydrated in cold water
- 7 oz soft tofu (½ block), drained and cut into ½ inch cubes
- 3 tablespoons shiro miso (white) or a combination of red and white miso, 2 tablespoons white, 1 tablespoon red
- 2 scallions, white and green parts thinly sliced

INSTRUCTIONS

- Bring the water or vegetable stock to a boil. Add the Takii or shiitake mushroom powder, if using. Add at least 1 cup of vegetables and reduce to a simmer. Cook vegetables for 3 minutes.
- In the meantime, mix the 3 tablespoons of miso paste with 1/4 cup of the heated stock from the pot. Add this mixture to the simmering stock and vegetables.
- Add the tofu and cook for 30 seconds. Drain the wakame, (squeeze it to remove excess water and chop it into ½ inch pieces) and add it and the scallions and cook for another 30 seconds.
- Remove the pot from the heat and serve. Sprinkle with more thinly sliced scallions and shichimi togarashi (7 spice pepper powder).

Japanese Rice

INGREDIENTS

I use Hitomebore or Tamanashiki brands

- 2 cups rice
- 2 cups water

INGREDIENTS

- 5-10 ounces of washed spinach or baby spinach
- ½ teaspoon low sodium soy sauce
- ¼ teaspoon Ume plum vinegar
- Sprinkle of Eden Shake

INSTRUCTIONS

- Rinse rice well. Drain in a strainer for 10 minutes.
- Place in the rice cooker or a pot and add 2 cups of water. Soak the rice for 15-20 minutes.
- Cook according to rice cooker instructions or if using stovetop, bring to a boil, reduce to low and cook for 15-20 minutes. Reduce the heat as low as possible and simmer for 5 more minutes. turn off and let sit without lifting the lid for 15 minutes.

Japanese Spinach

INSTRUCTIONS

• Fill a large bowl with water and add a cup of ice cubes. Set aside.

• Bring 6 quarts of water to a boil. Add washed spinach or baby spinach. Cook for 20-30 seconds and scoop them out and into a bowl of ice water.

• When cool, drain the spinach in a colander.

• Squeeze the spinach with your hands until all the water is squeezed out. Place a small bundle (¼ cup) of the spinach in a shallow bowl and drizzle on soy sauce, Ume plum vinegar and a sprinkle of Eden Shake.

Japanese Breakfast Tofu

INGREDIENTS

- 1 (14 ounces) block of extra firm tofu, drained and pressed, cut into small cubes
- Juice of 1 lemon
- ¼ teaspoon ginger powder
- Pinch of kosher salt
- 1 tablespoon low sodium soy sauce

INSTRUCTIONS

- Toss the tofu with the lemon juice, ginger and salt.
- Place half the tofu in the air fryer at 375° for 10 minutes. Turn it over after 5 minutes. Cook it a little longer to make it crispy.
- Remove and set aside and cook the other half. You can also use a regular oven at 400° for 20 minutes or until crispy.

Natto

INGREDIENTS

1 serving

- 1 package Natto (soybeans)
- 1 tablespoon sliced scallions
- 1 teaspoon low sodium soy sauce
- ¼ teaspoon Takii mushroom powder
- 1 serving steamed Japanese or brown rice for serving

INSTRUCTIONS

- Mix all ingredients together. Serve with rice

Natto is a nourishing fermented food made from soybeans. It is usually sold in the frozen section of Asian stores in single serving containers. It defrosts very quickly, so I take it out a few minutes before I need it. My mother would eat it over a bowl of hot Japanese rice. If you're not a fan of Natto and want a soybean dish for breakfast, just make one of the tofu dishes in this book. Any of them go well with the Japanese breakfast. In the photo, there is a photo of Tofu Bacon. I make Japanese rice occasionally, but brown rice is actually a better option since it's whole grain.

YOU CAN STAY UP TO DATE WITH CHEF JULIA HERE

Contact me: juliadunaway@gmail.com

My supplies can be found in my Amazon store.
As an Amazon Associate, I earn from qualifying purchases.
https://www.amazon.com/shop/chefjuliadunaway

Please subscribe to my YouTube Channel
https://www.youtube.com/watch?v=aLGwdCz2aFk

Website http://chef-julia.com/

Instagram
https://www.instagram.com/juliadunaway/?hl=en

Facebook
https://www.facebook.com/chefjuliadunaway/

Chef Julia Support Group & the Chef Julia 21 Day Challenge
https://www.facebook.com/groups/1986506241637015/

Made in the USA
Las Vegas, NV
29 September 2022